The House of Horrors

Also available from Windwhistle Press

San Francisco Ghosts
By Mark Lyon

The Grey Ghost Book
By Jessie Adelaide Middleton

Another Grey Ghost Book
By Jessie Adelaide Middleton

The White Ghost Book
By Jessie Adelaide Middleton

The House of Horrors

Leap Castle
The Most Haunted Castle
in
Ireland

Mildred Darby

Windwhistle Press

INTRODUCTION
by
Mark Lyon

When the independent-minded, rebellious and highly talented twenty year old Mildred Henrietta Gordon Dill (known as Milly to her friends) married the thirty-five year old Jonathon Charles Darby on the 7th of November, 1889 and moved into Leap Castle (pronounced lĕp) near Roscrea, in County Offaly, Ireland, she had every reason to believe that she could look forward to a delightfully bucolic happily ever after.

In the words of the county's *Midland Tribune* under the headline, "Rejoicings at Leap Castle": "Over the hall door hung the Irish motto *céad míle fáilte* (a hundred thousand welcomes) while the numerous lights of the castle shone out brilliantly.

"On each window were placed horse shoes to bring good luck and to keep away ghosts, for Leap Castle has hosts of traditions, even of ghosts. Arriving at the foot of the hill, the carriage of Mr. Darby and his bride was drawn home by the cheering tenantry, while a band of musicians gave full merriment to the scene and thus were the bride and the bridegroom drawn to the threshold of their home, one of the oldest in Hibernia."

Milly's joy, however, was to be short lived. Jonathon Darby was an arrogant autocrat with a violent temper remembered locally for upsetting his wife by often intentionally tracking in mud and muck from the stables onto her clean floors and by his family for the Christmas Day meal on which he erupted into such a fit of anger upon discovering that the maid had put the cold plates meant for the ham in front of the turkey and the hot plates meant for the turkey by the ham that he violently smashed the offending plates onto the floor and demanded that new plates be brought to him. It was only a matter of time before the marriage began to founder and, though they were to successfully raise four children (their first son dying in early infancy,) their union consisted of a never-ending battle of wills.

Particularly vexing to Jonathon was Milly's writing career. Writing under the pen name, Andrew Merry, by the year 1910, she had already published numerous short stories and three well reviewed novels when Jonathon, said to have been "wild with rage" at what he considered to be tales of "purple passion," forbade her to, ever again, set pen to paper for public consumption.

Arguably the most upsetting to Jonathon of all of her literary works was the story, "A House of Horrors," published in 1898 in *Belgravia: A London Magazine* and which was later republished in a longer and more detailed form along with an introduction attesting to the truthfulness of the account retitled, "Kilman Castle, The House of Horror," in the December 1908 issue of *The Occult Review*. It is this later version which I have republished here.

Although clothed in the guise of a fictional narrative by Andrew Merry with all of the names changed (Leap Castle being called Kilman Castle while Jonathon and Milly are called Maurice and Betty O'Connoll and the family name of the early lords of Leap being changed from O'Carroll to O'Connoll) it was obvious to those in the know that Milly's story was an alarmingly full and candid account of the ghostly goings on at Leap Castle. When Jonathon became aware of the story he was furious and it is said that he never forgave Milly for writing and publishing it. He always claimed that the ghost stories, which had been told for centuries about his much loved home, were sheer nonsense and he had absolutely forbidden Milly from speaking of them. "The only spirits in this house," he would often state in a voice which brooked no dissension, "are in the cellars!"

But, despite Jonathon's protestations, the ghosts and the incidents recounted in "The House of Horror" *were* real. Others had attested to ghostly encounters at Leap for ages and, though, perhaps, a trifle melodramatic in the telling, Milly's story was based upon fact. As the editor of *The*

8

Occult Review put it in his introduction to the piece, the author of the account "has herself witnessed on a number of different occasions the majority of the phenomena recorded. Though the narrative takes the form of a story, the incidents — I have her authority for stating — are in every instance vouched for as correct in fact and detail." And Milly, herself, had twice come face to face with the most terrifying of all the castle's supernatural entities, what she called "It" and "The Thing" and which others have termed "The Elemental."

"I was standing in the Gallery looking down at the main floor, when I felt somebody put a hand on my shoulder," she was to recall. "The thing was about the size of a sheep. Thin, gaunt, shadowy ... its face was human, to be more accurate, inhuman. Its lust in its eyes, which seemed half decomposed in black cavities, stared into mine. The horrible smell one hundred times intensified came up into my face, giving me a deadly nausea. It was the smell of a decomposing corpse."

She was to later describe a final encounter with "It" in a letter to a friend by the name of Sydney Carroll. "On the 25th November 1915," she disclosed, "two of our servants knowing the 'master' would be late and that I was driving that afternoon had invited 'friends' two soldiers from the Barracks at Birr distant the other side six miles. They came rather late and my husband came home early so the visitors had to be kept out of his sight in the lower regions of one of the wings (the Priest's House) and were unable to be shown the centre tower — the very lofty hall. At 7:15 my husband and I went up to dress for dinner, my room in extremity of house from kitchens, his dressing room next door to me.

"Whilst dressing I was startled by a loud yell of terror stricken male and female voices coming apparently from the hall — and ran out to see the cause. My husband was out ahead of me at his heels. I passed through corridor of the wing and onto the gallery .... On the gallery leaning with 'hands' resting on its rail I saw the Thing – the Elemental and smelt it only too well. At the same moment my husband pulled up sharply about ten feet from the Thing, and half turning let fly a volley of abuse at me ending up 'Dressing up a thing like that to try and make a fool of me. And now you'll say I've seen something and I have not seen anything and there is nothing to see, or ever was.' This last speech without a pause, begun waving one hand at the Thing end up by stalking back to his dressing room still abusing me for trying to give him a fright. As he was speaking the Elemental grew fainter and fainter in its outlines until it disappeared. By the sounds from my husband's room I judged he was employed as I was myself in preparing an empty spot for our coming dinner. He never made any enquiry as to the yell that called us both out, and from that day to this has not mentioned the incident to me.

"I heard from our servants that when we went to dress for dinner they had brought their friends just to show them the hall, when all four had suddenly seen and smelt the Elemental looking down at them from the gallery. They all got such a turn, they couldn't help letting out a bawl then fled to servants quarters where all four were very sick."

The next day the two maids presented Milly with letters claiming it was necessary for them to immediately pay visits to their homes. They never returned to Leap.

Following the publication of "The House of Horror" in *The Occult Review*, three letters from former houseguests attesting to their first-hand encounters with supernatural entities during their stays at the castle were sent to Milly who, then, forwarded them on to *The Occult Review*. In order to maintain the anonymity of the castle and its owners and to keep consist with the pseudonyms used in Milly's account, when these letters were printed in *The Occult Review*, the name of the castle was changed from Leap to Kilman and Jonathan Darby was identified as O'Connoll. However, in reprinting these letters here, I have replaced the pseudonyms with the real names.

"You have asked me to write down just what happened last night when you, with my brother and myself, had just come in from listening to the dogs making a tremendous barking and howling at half-past eleven," wrote one houseguest.

"When we came into the big hall I had my arm round your waist, and it was a sudden start that you gave made me look at your face.

"I saw your eyes fixed upon something above our heads, and the next minute my own eyes were filled by the sight of a Thing in the gallery looking down at us. There was plenty of light from the lamps in the hall, and the one above on the wall at the corner of the gallery, for every one of us to see quite plainly the grey-coloured figure about the height of a small grown-up person looking down at us. I wish I thought I could ever forget the sight of that grey figure with dark spots like holes in its head instead of eyes, standing with grey arms folded on the gallery railing looking down at us. It was the cry I gave in my horror made my brother look up too, and without waiting a second you remember he said, 'Stand here you two, and I will run round and upstairs to the gallery just to see who that joker is. I'll teach him to dress up like that to try and give you ladies a fright.'

"You and I stood just where we were, and neither of us said a word. Our eyes were fixed on the Thing — at least I know mine were and never shifted. I heard the rushing footsteps of my brother as he ran upstairs, and the opening of the gallery door. Then just as he put foot on the gallery, the Thing that he saw there, that we were watching, suddenly faded out of sight. The Thing did not move, only became less and less visible, until it vanished.

"My brother searched the gallery for any trace or sign of the figure we had all three seen, but found nothing.

"I only wish you would come away with us today. I do not like leaving you in this weird place, where I personally could not summon courage to remain another night."

Another former houseguest wrote of his encounter with the castle's "Red Lady."

"I have been asked to commit to paper the details of an occurrence that took place whilst I was on my first visit to Leap, the home of my old friend, Jonathon Darby. I gladly do this because although there is nothing very remarkable in the facts when viewed by themselves, nothing of a similar

14

or kindred nature has ever been experienced by me before. Also at the actual time I was deeply impressed. I arrived at Leap on the morning of the twentieth of October, 19—, perfectly sound and healthy in mind and body, certainly not a person accustomed to dream dreams or to start and shudder at a shadow. The days were spent in long tramps with dogs and gun after wild pheasants, snipe and rabbits, and the evenings in singing, reading and yarning, with games of Nap or Bridge; but beyond a casual remark or two I overheard made to my hostess about the castle being haunted, and with a description of three apparitions that a neighbour said he had seen in the dining room, nothing occurred at any time to cause me to think or to fancy that ghostly visitors were to be expected in my room, at any rate.

"On the thirty-first of October I went to my bedroom about 11:00 p.m., and before putting out my light I read over a very beautiful and semireligious ceremony which I had shortly to celebrate or conduct as 'Installing Master' of my Masonic Lodge. I am a very sound, steady sleeper, and yet am easily awakened by any unusual movement in my room at night. During the night, the time was 12:45 a.m., as I subsequently saw by my watch, I felt that I was awakened by somebody in my room. It was pitch dark and at first I could see nothing; I was wide awake with an extraordinary cold feeling at my heart that rapidly increased in intensity. Almost immediately I felt, as much as saw, that there was a tall figure in the, middle of the room. My first impression was that Darby himself was there, as no other member of the household would correspond to the height.

"'What is it?' I asked.

"There was no answer, but I now could see, dimly at first and then with increasing distinctness, that the tall figure was clothed from head to foot in red, and with its right hand raised menacingly in the air. To my utter astonishment I could see that the light which illuminated the figure was from *within*, having very much the effect of the dark lantern used in a photographer's room. As the figure advanced towards me the light increased, and I could see distinctly that the form was that of a very tall woman holding some sort of a weapon, knife or dagger, in her hand.

"'What is it?' I said again, adding, '*Who* is it?' and then hurriedly struck a match and lit my candle.

"As the flame of the match and candle illumined the room I looked all round. The room was empty. I jumped out of bed and carefully examined the curtains to see if by any chance the light from the window could have caused the effect above described, or if I could find any possible explanation. I put out the candle, and getting into bed again, carefully looked to see if in the dark I could account for what I had seen. No, the night was too black, and the curtains too closely drawn for any glimmering from without to filter in. Not satisfied, I relit the candle and made a systematic search round the room. I found everything in order, and my door locked, exactly as I had left it when going to bed. From the moment that I noticed that the light emanated *from* the figure I was convinced that what I saw was supernatural. Convinced, too, against my will, for up to this, I had been one of the greatest unbelievers in the possibility of apparitions or of spirits being seen. I can't say I felt exactly frightened, but more solemnly impressed. My pre-conceived opinions were utterly swept away, and I *knew* I had been face to face with something beyond my power to explain away.

"I went back to bed again, but decided that I must not fall asleep thinking of the 'scarlet woman,' or else I should be sure to dream of her, and I knew that what I had seen was not 'in a dream.' Accordingly I said over to myself some of my Masonic ritual, and then recalled the numerous 'shots' that I had missed during the day, and the picturesque language in which my host had expressed his opinion of me, but in a few minutes I again felt the bitter cold over or at my heart — I put my hand inside the breast of my pyjama jacket but found the flesh quite warm. I stared intently into the middle of the room but could see nothing. Presently the cold grip seemed to pass away. Again and again this occurred. Every time I was convinced that 'something' was there, but I could see and indeed saw nothing again. In about an hour's time I fell asleep and was not disturbed till the manservant 'called' me.

"As I prefaced this memoir, there is nothing very remarkable or thrilling in what I describe, but I know that I was not dreaming, that I saw a real 'unreality,' and that I was not the victim of a practical joke. Apparitions are not a subject for jest at Leap Castle either with host or guests."

A third houseguest wrote, "You want me to tell you exactly what occurred the first night I spent with you all at Leap last November. I went up to my room, which was in the Priest's House, called the ------- Room, and I liked my quarters very much. The great big beam across the ceiling was so old-fashioned and in keeping with the rest of the castle, as were the well-worn uncarpeted stairs outside leading down to the little hall and up to the top storey.

"Well, I went to bed quite happily, no thought of ghosts or any such things in my head, and soon was fast asleep.

"The next day when I came down to breakfast, you asked me, 'Had I slept well?' And you may remember I told you I had been a little disturbed and wakeful. When we were alone after breakfast, you asked me to tell you candidly what had given me a bad night, and I told you just what I now put down.

"You know that I was a perfect stranger to Leap and all its stories. Also I was quite ignorant as to the various apparitions other people had seen within its walls. As for expecting to see a spook myself, as one of those who pride themselves upon being strong, athletic, and well-trained, in perfect health without the knowledge of what nerves meant, I should have laughed at any one even suggesting I could see a ghost. Well, that first night I went to bed and to sleep at once, to be awakened later by a curious feeling of oppression — just as if some very heavy body was on my bed nearly pushing me out. Into my mind came the idea that one of the dogs had got into my room, and I put out my hand to feel over the bed clothes — but beyond a sensation as if I had plunged my hand into ice-cold water, there was nothing.

"As the weight on my bed did not move, I resolved to get out and light a candle — to look in fact, and see what was there. But the candle revealed nothing but a deep impression in the counterpane* next to the impression made between the sheets where my own body had just been.

"I tried to lift the bed-clothes right off the bed, but from the side where the impression was I could not shift them. So after many endeavours to account for what seemed unaccountable, I was driven to the conclusion that there really are stranger things in this world than my philosophy could explain, and rather than take my place next to that unseen heavy weight of mystery, I got a book and a cigarette, and did not try to get into bed again until the day broke. Then having opened the shutters and the windows, I once more went over to the bed — found the impression on the counterpane if anything deeper than when I held last looked, but on trying to lift the clothes I rejoiced to find that I could do so. The weight was gone — so I was back in my own place between the sheets when my cup of tea was brought to me.

"I have had further experiences, such as hearing footsteps, etcetera, when my eyes

*an expensive, often embroidered coverlet

told me there was no one visible to make the sounds, and all the time that I have been in Leap have felt that some one was trying to get recognition or communication with me. But to this thought I have never paid any attention, except to chase it out of my mind as quickly as possible, and to resolve each time it returned more strongly, that I would not be the means if I could avoid it for the Unseen inhabitants of your old home to make themselves more troublesome than they do at present, by taking messages or encouraging them to attempt communication.

"I only wish I knew of some one who has studied the Unseen enough to be able to come to Leap and make its invisible occupants go to the rest that they, I suppose, are seeking — which they certainly prevent you and plenty of other living people from getting."

In letters to Carroll, Milly wrote of being awakened in the middle of the night by groans and hearing "something very heavy" fall to the floor of "Murder Hole Room" adjoining her bedroom. Upon investigation she found that nothing had fallen from the walls but, upon stepping on a normally dry dark stain on the old oaken floorboards, the stain was now "warm and moist" and that her foot had become stained with blood.

She also related to Carroll how all of her children had reported seeing the ghosts until they reached the age of four or five. "None of them exhibited any sign of fear, speaking with interest and curiosity of what they saw," she wrote. "They usually spoke enquiring as to who were the lovely lady in red, the funny old man in black with such a shiny head, the little man in green clothes with such beautiful shining things on his shoes, all alike, and sometimes two together saw these."

In a letter written to St. John D. Seymour for inclusion in his book, *True Irish Ghost Stories*, Milly wrote, "When first we went there we heard people talking, but on looking everywhere we could find no one. Then on some nights we heard fighting in the glen beside the house. We could hear voices raised in anger, and the clash of steel: no person would venture there after dusk.

"One night I was sitting talking with my governess, I got up, said good-night, and opened the door, which was on the top of the back staircase. As I did so, I heard some one (a woman) come slowly upstairs, walk past us to a window at the end of the landing, and then with a shriek fall heavily. As she passed it was bitterly cold, and I drew back into the room, but did not say anything, as it might frighten the governess.

"She asked me what was the matter, as I looked so white. Without answering, I pushed her into her room, and then searched the house, but with no results.

"Another night I was sleeping with my little girl. I awoke, and saw a girl with long, fair hair standing at the fireplace, one hand at her side, the other on the chimney-piece. Thinking at first it was my little girl, I felt on the pillow to see if she were gone, but she was fast asleep. There was no fire or light of any kind in the room.

"Some time afterwards a friend was sleeping there, and she told me that she was pushed out of bed the whole night. Two gentlemen to whom I had mentioned this came over, thinking they would find out the cause. In the morning when they came down they asked for the carriage to take them to the next train, but would not tell what they had heard or seen.

"Another person who came to visit her sister, who was looking after the house before we went in, slept in this room, and in the morning said she must go back that day. She also would give no information.

"On walking down the corridor, I have heard a door open, a footstep cross before me, and go into another room, both doors being closed at the time. An old cook I had told me that when she went into the hall in the morning, a gentleman would come down the front stairs, take a plumed hat off the stand, and vanish through the hall door. This she saw nearly every morning. She also said that a girl often came into her bedroom, and put her hand on her (the cook's) face; and when she would push her away she would hear a girl's voice say, 'Oh don't!' three times. I have often heard voices in the drawing-room, which decidedly sounded as if an old gentleman and a girl were talking. Noises like furniture being moved were frequently heard at night, and strangers staying with us have often asked why the servants turned out the rooms underneath them at such an unusual hour. The front door bell sometimes rang, and I have gone down, but found no one."

When, in 1916, Jessie Adelaide Middleton reprinted "The House of Horror" in her classic collection of true tales of the supernatural, *The White Ghost Book,* she prefaced the account with the following statement:

"For this weird ghost-story — a story which, for sheer horror, is hard to beat — I am indebted to the writer, Andrew Merry, from whom, by way of further testimony to the story's truth, I have just received a letter, in which occur these words: 'Since it was written as much again of facts could be added to it, including the seeing of the grey Elemental last November by five people, beside myself, at the same time.'"

In early 1922 Jonathon found himself at odds with his tenants which resulted in their refusal to pay their rents and their implementing a boycott against the Darbys.

When events escalated to the point that, on several occasions, shots were fired through the castle windows and their garden was destroyed by persons unknown, in April or May of that year the Darbys felt compelled to flee from their home and live with their daughter in Longford. "We were forced to leave with only a few clothes leaving all our precious belongings behind us," Milly later confided to a friend.

Early on the morning of Sunday, July 30th 1922, an unidentified group of eleven men broke into the castle and, after smashing the furniture into what could be utilized as firewood, they set the castle on fire destroying both the center and the northern portions of the castle. The next morning the previously untouched southern part of the castle was also set ablaze as locals looked on and looted whatever could be salvaged from the fire.

Having been alerted that something like this might occur, Jonathon had, previous to the fire, made trips to the castle and removed his books and other valuables to a safe house. Milly, however, lost all of her clothing, jewelry, books and, most terrible of all, the manuscripts for over one hundred and fifty unpublished stories and two unpublished novels; the creative output of thirty years for, despite Jonathon's demand that she never again publish, she had never stopped writing.

For decades the castle remained an ominous burned out ruin, often referred to as "The Most Haunted Castle in Ireland." Local lore has it that, in the course of an argument with a man concerning the castle ghost stories, Jonathon offered to give the man a thousand pounds if he could endure twelve nighttime hours alone in the castle ruins. It is said that after spending only a little more than an hour in the castle, he fled in terror, refusing to ever disclose what he had encountered.

In 1974 Peter Bartlett, an Australian with Irish roots, purchased the ruins and enthusiastically set about restoring both the castle and the gate lodge.

Following Bartlett's death in 1989, the castle was bought by the musician Seán Ryan, renowned throughout the world as a virtuoso tin whistle player. Seán continued the restoration of the castle and he has brought much of the central tower back to its original medieval glory.

Seán, his wife Anne, a well known teacher of Irish dance, and their daughter, Ciara, a talented musician and championship Irish dancer in her own right, moved into the castle and the family has had their own ghostly experiences. Seán has spoken of a hooded figure being seen and whispering being heard in what is called "The Bloody Chapel" comprising the top floor of the tower as well as encounters with a phantom lady in Victorian attire whom Seán believes might be a governess and two ghostly little girls referred to as Charlotte and Emily. On a recent visit to Leap, Seán told me that, from time to time, locals still report seeing an eerie light shining from within "The Bloody Chapel" when no one is up there.

Fortunately, while recent visitors speak, at times, of experiencing an inexplicable sense of terror and of smelling a foul sulfurous odor, the Elemental has not been reported to have been seen in all of its horrific hideousness since the departure of the Darbys.

KILMAN CASTLE

The House of Horror

By

Andrew Merry

This story regarding an Irish castle, which I have named Kilman Castle, calls for some special explanation — which, personally, I am unable to give. Perhaps amongst the younger generation of scientists — who can tabulate and dissect anything, and by analysis explain anything — one will be found to undertake the task of reducing the apparitions at this house of horror to their original elements, but the task is beyond me. I can merely write down the facts as they came to my knowledge.

Two of the people who have seen the elemental apparition here recorded, and the "Captain Gordon" in whose name this tale is told, passed out of this world of speculation very soon after their vision of the uncanny spook.

Fully realizing the howls of incredulous laughter with which critics will greet this confession, I here declare that on three separate occasions I have personally verified some of the experiences related, and that twice I saw the Elemental. Since that vision two very serious accidents have taken me to the gates of the next world — indeed, almost through them. Andrew Merry

CHAPTER I

This is a true story of facts that have occurred, and that are occurring.

I admit at once that my tale will be deemed improbable, even impossible. Still, a number of men and women, many of them living, have seen and heard the things I am about to relate. Of course, you may assume that they were all the victims of hysterical delusions, that it is all a matter of auto-telepathic hypnotic suggestion, or any other sonorous collection of syllables you please to string together; but that these things were seen and heard by healthy, intelligent people, and are still seen and heard, is indisputable.

For myself, I do not fancy I am a neurotic, or have a highly strung imaginative temperament. I am a captain in a native Indian regiment, thirty-two years of age, sound in wind and limb, and generally "grass" what I aim at, so imagine my eyesight is not faulty. I have done a good share of active service, and can honestly say I never felt nervous in my life before the month of November last year when I was staying with my cousin at Kilman Castle, near the west coast of Ireland.

Looking back on the whole matter, now that some months have passed, I am still unable to find any possible explanation of this impossible story.

I shall therefore just relate it exactly as it occurred, with all the details of my visit, so that any one who in the future may read this record, may be able to put himself in my place and visualize somewhat the surroundings, and the people in the midst of whom the facts I am going to relate occurred, and indeed are still occurring.

When I arrived at the railway station of the small Irish county town named Ballykinkope, the daylight of the short November day was gradually sinking into twilight.

A grey-headed porter opened the carriage door and collected my gun-case, rugs and golf-clubs.

"Another bag in the van? Right, sorr! Will yer 'anner be wanting a kyar? "he inquired. "Where will ye be going to?"

"To Kilman Castle," I replied.

"Then 'twill be you are Captain Gordon that the Castle kyar is just afther comin' for. This way, sorr."

He led me out of the wooden building doing duty as station offices to where a tall dog-cart was waiting, and soon my luggage was stowed away. A wizened little old groom seated himself beside me, driving the raking sixteen-hand horse at a good pace along the greasy road.

"That's a nice traveller," I remarked, nodding in the direction of the horse, and noting the long, easy stride.

"He is that same, sorr. His sire was 'Stupendous,' Lord Brosna's cilibrated American trotter," answered the old man.

Then he added respectfully, touching his hat, "'Twill be your first sight of the Castle, I think, Captain?"

The man was right. As a matter of fact, I was in Ireland for the first time. Since my cousin had married Maurice O'Connoll, the owner of Kilman Castle, I had not been in England, spending my leave in various hunting and shooting expeditions nearer to my regiment in India.

When at last I had come back to London, I found, amongst the letters welcoming me, one from Betty, telling me to pack up my gun, golf-clubs and fishing-rods, to bring plenty of riding clothes, and to start "at once" for Kilman.

She added: —

"You may as well be prepared to take up your abode in Ireland. I have got a dimpled Irish girl for you with a delightful dot — the last a rarity nowadays in this distressful country. So be ready for the worst."

I needed no inducements of "dimples "or "dots," for after my long spell in India, the idea of the Green Isle was attraction enough.

"You've been with the O'Connolls some time, I suppose?" I asked my ancient Jehu; he had the air and manners of a confidential servant.

"Wid the mashter, and the ould man before him, sorr. I drove the mashter to his christenin', an' I drove him an' the mishtress home when he first brought her from England, an', plase God, I'll live to drive thim to their funeral yit, for there's years of work in this arrum." He spoke in perfect good faith, with tones of the utmost devotion to "the mashter," whose early demise he thus anticipated.

"Shure, it was great divarshuns we had that time," he continued, "when the mashter married — bonfires an' dancing, lashings of porther, and of potheen, all through the night. It took me an' the steward all our time to git the gintlemen, who had taken a sup too much, safe out of the ring before the family was up the next morning."

"Kilman is a very old place, I think?"

"It is that same, sorr, an' none older round these parts at all, at all. There's been many a bloody battle fought near by, an' for that matther, there's one livin' now as was hid in the Castle when the Ribbon boys — God rest their sowls — were about."

"You've had wild times enough in Ireland often," I said encouragingly, hoping to get him to talk freely. He needed little inducing, and continued —

"That's a fact, sorr. 'Tis often I've heard of my gran'father's gran'father, an' his doings wid the Wild Captain O'Connoll. I can just remind me of my gran'father's telling us the tales — him an ould, ould man, no one knew what age — just as his gran'father tould them to himself. There's one sthory — but belike I'm wearying you wid my talk, sorr."

I reassured him, and he started again.

"Well, sorr, they do say that the Wild Irish had besieged the Castle, and were afther burning the O'Moore's house up beyant the Knockganoc. The Wild Captain an' his Yeomen — he had a troop three hundred strong, which did more against the rapparrees than all the King's soldiers put together — was shut up tight in the Castle, wid three or four thousand of the mountain men camped round in the plain. The Maw Goughlal was commanding the rapparrees, a mighty robber chief he was, an' him an' the Wild Captain had many a grudge to sittle whin the saints brought thim together. Well, whin the Wild Captain heard that the Maw had burnt the O'Moore's house over his head, an' killed th' ould man, an' more too, takin' Miss Diana O'Moore a prisoner, the Captain wint mad wid rage; for by that token he was thinkin' that the Lily of Avaghoe, as Miss O'Moore was named, would have made a wife for himself. 'Twas said her father had a power of goulden guineas and precious stones, hid up in a big brass pot, for a marriage gift for her. '

"So by this an' that the Captain fairly was rale wild, an' he rushed to where his Yeomen were feasting an' cried out aloud —

"'Who will risk his life wid me to save the Lily of Avaghoe?"

38

"Wid a shout you could hear at Croaghaun, every man answered him —

"'Tis meself will!"

"The Wild Captain smiled, and they did be saying a dozen rapparrees had betther be savin' their sowls, whinever he smiled.

"'Come thin,' he says, an' the gates were opened an' they rode out an' fought the Irishers all the day, slaughtering frightful!

"But though they killed an' killed, an' though the Wild Captain's grey horse come home crimson to the saddle-flaps, not one sight did they git of the Lily of Avaghoe, before the twilight come on. So they turned sorrowful into the Cassle.

"The Wild Captain ate no mate, but sat wid his head bint, not one daring to pass the time o' day wid him.

"At last he sint for my gran'father's gran'father.

"'Teighe,' says he, 'will ye come to the gates of hell wid me?'

"'I will that same,' says my gran'father's gran'father, 'an' that skippin'.'

"'Thin git the clothes off two of them carrion, an' be quick.'

"So the other he got two set of the mountain men's clothes, an' the two of them put them on, an' disguised themselves as strolling beggars, one wid pipes an' the other wid a fiddle. Thin they left the castle unbeknownst to any one but a sintry.

"'Teighe,' says the Wild Captain, "if the rapparrees dishcover us we're dead men.'

"'They'll kill us for sartain,' agrees my gran'father's gran'father, 'an' more times than not roast us alive, when we're dead first.'

"'They'll be apt to be thousands to one agin us.'

"'Or more, Captain, the Lord be praised!'

"'Teighe, ye can go back now, and not one sowl think the worse of ye.'

"'Shure ye know I'd die for you, captain dear, an' if it's hell you're bound for, it's meself will be thare first, wid the door open for yer honour. Is it me 'ud renaigh?"

"So no more passed between them until they reached the mountains.

"'It's Irish we'll spake,' whispered the Captain, whin they saw the light of the ribbel fires. Thin they hailed the sintry in Irish, telling him they had escaped the English, an' soon both were warmin' their hands to the fire an' ateing from the big pot that hung over that same.

"After supper, they played an' sang ribil songs an' ould haythenish Irish tunes, an' my gran'father's gran'father said the Wild Captain made his fiddle spake; whilst himself, he put his sowl into the pipes, until the mountain men wint wild wid delight at the grand tunes of them.

"'It's to the Maw they must play,' the ribils cried, an' soon the two was led further up into the mountains, where the Maw and fourteen of his chieftains sat — an' there right in the middle of the ribil lot, wid her two pretty hands and her two little fate tied wid a coarse bit of rope, lay the Lily of Avaghoe safe enough.

"Then the two played and sung to the Maw, until he grew tired and felt like slapeing.

""'Tis well you're here,' says the Maw. 'Ye will play at my widding to-morra; 'an' he grinned as he looked at the prisoner.

""'We will that same, an' dance too,' cried the Wild Captain, smiling up in his face.

""'Twill be the English will dance,' growled the Maw, 'wid no ground under their feet. I'll make hares of them the day.'

"An' wid this he tould thim how 'twas all planned to surprise the Castle at the break o' day, an' how one of the most trusted of the yeomen had agreed to open a door where he would be sintry, in exchange for Mr. O'Moore's pot of gould and treasure.

""'Tis a foine skame,' cried the Wild Captain, 'an' worthy of the Maw Goughlal. But if it's for the break o' day, shure 'tis slape you'd best be gettin', for it's only three hours off the dawning now.'

"So they all lay round the fires to slape; the Maw an' the fourteen of his chiefs and the two beggars round the one fire, an' the rest of the army a little dishtance off.

"The fires died down a bit, and barrin' a sob or two from the Lily of Avaghoe, nothing stirred or spoke.

"Thin my gran'father's gran'father felt a long knife thrust in his hand, an' the Wild Captain whispered to him —

"'Split their throats from ear to ear, that they may not cry out. Cut deep.'

"Slowly the two of them crept around, pausing at each slapeing rapparree, an' littin' his ribil blood flow out on the grass.

"Not one of the fifteen as much as turned over; the Captain killed eight, an' the Maw, an' my gran'father's gran'father killed the rest.

"'Be silint, Diana, me darlint,' whispered the Wild Captain to the Lily of Avaghoe. 'We've come to save you.' Wid that he cut the ropes that bound her, an' telling her to follow him, he crept out of the firelight, she after him, an' my gran'father's gran'father lasht of all.

"The Captain he knew every fut of them mountains, so did me gran'father's gran'father, and skirtin' round the rapparrees' camp, they reached the Castle in safety. You may be sure, sorr, it wasn't long before the Captain had his yeomen out, and they attacked the ribils still sleepin' in their camp, an' slaughtered a thousand or more before the sun was well up."

"But what became of the treacherous sentry?" I asked.

"Shure he danced — in the air — at the Wild Captain's widding wid Miss O'Moore."

"And what became of the pot of treasure?"

"Shure the Captain he took that wid his lady, an' they do say —"

44

"Well?"

"Ah! — it's only the country talk, yer 'anner, but they do say the crock of gould is buried somewhere in or near the Castle. Ye see, it fell out this way; the Wild Captain and the English King didn't agree about some little matther, an' the English King sint the ridcoats to besiege the Castle. Now the Castle has a long underground passage between it an' a rath on the hill near by. In this rath, all the cattle an' bastes were kept, an' driven down the passage whin they were wanted. Well, the ridcoats dug an' found the passage an' stopped it up wid big rocks an' such like, so they in the Castle had ne'er a bit or sup for three days. Then the Wild Captain in the night he called two serving men, and says he to them —

"'Help me to carry this ould crock of butter.'

"But what he called the crock of butter was the big brass pot full of gould and jewils. 'Twas as much as the three could do to carry it. So whin they got to the shpot the Wild Captain had chosen, they dug a hole an' buried it. Then they all three wint

45

together to the top of the Castle to look at the English below them.

"'Fergus,' says the Wild Captain to wan of the serving men, 'go down an' bring me my sword from my room; 'tis meself will test it afore to-morrow's battle.'

"So Fergus, he wint. Thin the Wild Captain he says to the other, 'Kiernan, do ye remimber where we hid the ould crock o' butter?"

"'I do, O'Connoll,' says Kiernan; "twas there an' there we put the gould.'

"'May your sowl rist wid it,' says the Wild Captain, an' wid that he knocked him over the edge of the battlemints an' on to his skull on the top of the English ridcoats on the stones below.

"When Fergus brought up the sword the Wild Captain made pretince of trying the edge wid his finger.

"'Are ye sure ye sharpened it well?' says he.

"'I am,' answers Fergus.

"'Thin may it sind your sowl to paradise this minute;' an' wid that he chops off the head of him an' throws him over the walls too.

"Thin the Wild Captain, rather than die like a rat in a hole, giv' himself up, an' they took him to Dublin, and condemned him, along with Sir William O'Brien — a grand gintleman livin' sivin miles beyant — to be hung, drawn and quartered for treason."

"What an ignominious ending for Captain O'Connoll," I observed.

"Oh! they did not hang him, sorr. The King was frighted when all was said an' done, so both gintlemin were pardoned. But they had put such heavy irons on the Captain's legs, that he never could walk again, and he died away, not clare in his mind. Whin he lay dyin' he towld the sthory of the gould to ease his sowl, but no one could ever find the place he meant, tho' they dug, an' dug, an' dug. Ah, but it's just a sthory! There, sorr, now we can see the Cassle'," pointing with his whip to a grey square tower showing over the tops of the leafless trees.

Kilman Castle was a sombre-looking bare building, consisting of a square keep tapering slightly to the top, looking in its grim grey strength, as if it could defy time itself. Flanking it on each side were wings of more modern build, and beyond one wing was a curious rambling-looking house, which my driver told me was called "The Priest's House," and which evidently had at one time been quite apart from the Castle, though now part and parcel of the house, being connected by one of the wings. Even the trees round seemed to grow in gaunt, weird shapes, probably because their tops caught the full blast of the wind, and their branches creaked and groaned above our heads as we passed under their overhanging shadows.

The gateway was castellated and overgrown with lichens and creepers, and the drive bordered with ancient walls, beyond them the ruins of other old walls or buildings, all overgrown and covered with moss and ferns. Even the topmost branches of the big sycamores were decorated with these same ferns, which grew in endless profusion in every niche and corner.

"'Twill be a wild night," my driver remarked, pointing to the murky red sky showing through the trees. As he spoke, a loud mournful cry sounded above us and was repeated three times.

I started at the first cry, then laughed, for I quickly recognized the noise to be the call of the hoot owl. Often had I heard these birds in India and seen my native servants cower panic-stricken, for in some parts of the East the cry of an owl is regarded as a token of coming death to one of the hearers.

"That's a loud voiced customer," I said. "Are there many of his feather round here?"

"No, Captain; we never had but that one of scracheing kind. He was here all the summer, an' now the winter do be comin' on, he's spoiling the thrade of Matt's shebeen beyant at the crassroads by the same token."

"How on earth can an owl spoil the trade of a public house?"

"'Tis the mountain min mostly, sorr, goes there, an' ne'er a mother's son of them will put fut outside their cabins afther dark since that gintlemin in the ivy has been hooting. They mountain fellars be rale skeared, for they do be believin' in pishrogues an' such like, an' they do be sayin' 'tis an evil spirit keening for a sowl that will die near by. There have been a power o' wakes lately — what wid the influenzy, an' the ould folks been pinched wid the cowld — in a good hour be it spoken! Here we are, sorr."

A bright light shone through the opened door, and in the warm welcome that Betty and her good man gave me I forgot the bleak night, the hooting owl, and the bloodthirsty traditions the voluble groom had been telling me.

CHAPTER II

The interior of Kilman Castle is quite in keeping with its weather-worn outer walls. I may as well describe it now, though it was not until the next morning that I went over the place with Maurice O'Connoll.

The entrance hall is very lofty, with a gallery running round three sides, and is paved with black and white stones. The walls are pierced — evidently long after they were originally built — by archways leading into the two wings, and are twenty feet thick. They are honeycombed with narrow passages, and at two corners of the tower are circular stone staircases, fine bits of rough-hewn masonry, each wedge-shaped step resting on its fellows; both staircases are as perfect as the day they were built. It was curious to me to note how the inner axles of these winding ladder-like stairs had had the blackened stones polished smooth and bright by the many generations of hands that had pressed against them, as their owners ran up and down these primitive ways.

O'Connoll told me that tradition states that the Castle was originally built by the Irish for the Danes, who seemed to have extracted forced labour from the half-clad barbarians before Ireland was fully christianized. The story whispered by the country folk declares that the mortar used in its construction was made in a great measure with human blood and human hair, and that therefore it has withstood the ravages of time. Somewhere about the year 800 the Irish, under the leadership of a chieftain named O'Connoll, rose against their oppressors, and took possession of the Castle, where O'Connoll established himself, and soon became a powerful prince. His descendants inhabited this Castle, whether the original building, or a more modern one built of the materials and on the site of the old one, history does not reveal; and until the advent of the English in the fifteenth and sixteenth centuries, this stronghold was considered impregnable. Amongst the first of the English adventurers was a young squire — son of an English knight — who hoped to win his spurs at the expense of the wild Irish. The expedition he was attached to, attracted by the rumour of the O'Connoll's riches, besieged the Castle, and in a sortie the defenders made, the young squire was taken prisoner. He was confined in a little room off one of the staircases, and as all the Irish were very busy defending the Castle, the only daughter of the house, one Finnueguolla O'Connoll, was deputed to push what food they allowed the prisoner through a little hole in the walls of his dungeon.

The Englishman made the best use of his opportunity, and by judiciously tender speeches, he succeeded in winning the maiden so completely to his side that one day, with a view of abetting his escape, she procured the key of the prison and let him out. As he was running down the twisting staircase, he met young O'Connoll, the girl's only brother, coming up, who immediately raised a hue and cry. The escaping prisoner turned and fled upward, eventually coming out on to the battlements of the tower. Seeing that flight any other way was impossible, and preferring the risk of sudden death to the more lingering one his attempted escape would ensure him, were he to be recaptured, he gave a mighty jump over the parapet, and managed to find refuge, and not death, in the branches of a yew-tree growing near the walls, reaching his countrymen safely.

Eventually, his rather treacherous lover betrayed the Castle to the English; its inhabitants were all hung in a field — called to this day "The Hangman's Field" — and the English squire married Finnueguolla, taking her name and the lands of her father by right of marriage and conquest.

Their son, Maurice O'Connoll, was one of the first high sheriffs appointed in Ireland, and his tomb, dated 1601, is still to be seen in the little churchyard near Kilman.

The tower had originally five floors or stories; of these three exist — the first, a big bricked-up room, under the present hall; then the hall itself; and at the top of the tower a large chapel, with a fine east window and stone altar.

Besides the bricked-up room under the hall are dungeons hollowed out of the rock itself, with no windows or communication to the outer air, and some of which O'Connoll now used as wine cellars. In a corner of the chapel at the top of the tower is an *oubliette*, where disagreeable strangers were invited to walk down two steps on to a hinged platform that let them fall below the level of the deepest dungeon, where pointed stakes helped to give them a quick journey to the nether world.

"A couple of cartloads of old bones and bone dust were cleared out of that," my host told me, "and buried with due ceremony in the churchyard by some superstitious old ancestor of mine. Amongst others who were said to have been thrown down there was a priest, the brother of a far-back O'Connoll, who offended the reigning head of the family by beginning mass here one day without him. That particular prince was a beauty — one of his little games was getting a hundred and fifty mercenaries to help him fight the English, and when the enemy were beaten off, to avoid paying his hired friends, he treated them all to a poisoned feast in the hall here, and killed the whole lot! See these skulls and bits of bones? They came out of the wall when we made a new window. The idea is, that when this place was besieged, the garrison had no way of burying their dead, so they cemented the bodies up in the walls. That's one explanation; the other is the two-penny coloured 'walled up' alive business. You can pay your money and take your choice. Here, anyhow, are the skulls and bones that came out of the wall; I don't trouble my head how they got in there."

This rambling description will, I hope, give some idea of the environment of this story, and form the outlines of a mental picture of the quaint old place, which has been inhabited without a break for at least a thousand years.

As for the legends and stories belonging to it, their name is legion — all telling of love, murder, and rapine, as such medieval traditions are always wont to run.

CHAPTER III

My first evening at Kilman passed very quickly and pleasantly. Betty and I yarned over old times until my host passed from the passive remonstrance of ill-concealed yawns to more active measures, by saying rather sternly —

"Betty, Kenneth had no sleep last night, so we must pack him off early to-night. It's getting late — half-past eleven. There go the dogs!"

As he spoke, the baying of many dogs, "of high and low degree," broke into a noisy chorus, rising to a crescendo of angry fear, and then dying down into a pianissimo of canine woe.

The big deerhound, Oscar, who was lying on a sheepskin rug in the hall, added a long, deep note of misery to the general orchestra.

"Do those dogs see the moon?" I asked. "What a curious noise they make!"

"There isn't a moon to-night," O'Connoll answered. "But the dogs here always do that. It's one of their little ways that won't hear explaining. They mark half-past eleven without fail; we can set the clocks by them."

"Probably some shadow in the trees at that time," I hazarded.

"So I thought, and we shifted them to the other side of the place, but it was just the same over there. No, don't ask Betty about it, or she'll keep you up all night telling some cock-and-bull ghost story if you do. Now, once more will you go to bed, Betty? Think of that poor 'divil' of a maid waiting up for you all this time. Have a whisky and soda, Gordon, before turning in?"

Whilst we were consuming the wine of the country I asked O'Connoll if he knew of any ghost story connected with the Castle.

He looked at me curiously, and then laughed.

"A ghost? We've only a couple of dozen or more, my dear fellow. But surely you are not the cut of Spooky Believer? Don't tell me you take a 'Julia' or such-like familiar about with you!"

It was my turn to laugh now.

My host continued —

"I've been here all my life, often quite alone, and never have I seen what I can't quite explain to myself by natural causes — electricity, you know, and all that. Of course, there are noises enough, but what old house is free from them? It's only rats in a great measure. What I say is, that the only spirits about arise from the too liberal consumption of this spirit," he tapped the tantalus stand. "The servants get drinking — we've an old cook now who'd see you under the table, but her omelettes cover a multitude of sins — and then they kick up a row themselves, get frightened, swear they see ghosts, and clear off in a body next day. If anything makes me really mad, it's the rot people talk about spirits and apparitions in this house."

"What says Betty to all these things? Does she listen to such folly? Of all the women in the world, one would swear she would not."

My host pulled angrily at his pipe and enveloped himself in a cloud of smoke before he replied —

"She got some idiotic maggot in her brain last year, and has turned ever since as nervous as a cat. It's too bad of her; I did think she had some common sense — that was why I married her." This with the sublime disregard of any sentimentality common to Benedicts of some years standing. "Just now she has been worrying my life out, trying to get me to go away for this month; it is in November most of these mysterious follies are said to appear — because the nights are dark, I expect! Betty would die sooner than go upstairs alone at night. It's too provoking of her; I wish you'd chaff her into common sense again."

I did not believe for a minute that Betty was really nervous! She was certainly playing some deep-laid practical joke upon her husband. I mutely determined to be wary of turnip-headed bogies and booby

60

traps, for in the past my cousin had occasionally indulged in such childish follies.

We went up the broad oaken staircase in one of the wings, and then along the gallery overlooking the hall.

A funny little doorway in the wall, about the height of my shoulders, raised my curiosity; Maurice O'Connoll, taking advantage of his six feet and odd inches, pulled it open to show me the winding narrow staircase it concealed. A rush of cold air nearly put our lights out, and he hastily pushed the door to, which seemed very heavy.

"It's all iron-plated," he explained. "In the Rebellion of '98, the family, and, in fact, all the Protestants of the neighbourhood, took refuge in there. However, I won't begin telling you the legends. My wife is the best to do that; if she does not know an appropriate story, she invents one on the spot."

With this parting libel on Betty's veracity, he showed me my quarters, and after seeing

I had everything I needed, he wished me good-night and departed.

My room was a long narrow one, with a fireplace across one corner. The floor was of polished poplar, with a couple of rugs on it. To my delight I saw that instead of the ordinary heavy curtained bedstead one would picture as appropriate to the house, there was one of modern make, with a wire-wove mattress.

I locked my door as a precautionary measure against bogies — or practical joking — and began leisurely to divest myself of my clothes, when I became conscious of some one breathing heavily in the room.

"Hullo," I thought, "here is a hospitable spook manifesting at once for the credit of the house."

Then O'Connoll's remarks about the servant and whisky came back to me. Horrors! If it was the bibulous cook!

The breathing was now snoring, and came unmistakably from under the bed.

Seizing the poker I gave a vicious sweep with it, abjuring the snorer to "come out at once."

There was a patter of feet, and out crept an obese and aged fox-terrier of the feminine persuasion, showing her few remaining front teeth in an apologetic grin, and agitating her minimum of tail with cringing affability.

As the old lady seemed an amiable specimen of her race, and apparently had been recently washed with carbolic soap, I determined to allow her to be my guest for the night, even if she was self-invited. So I threw her my rug, which she proceeded to make into a bed for herself in a corner near the fireplace, scratching and turning round and round, and finally, with a grunt of satisfaction, curling into a ball, watching my toilet operations with brazen effrontery, and wagging her tail whenever she caught my eye.

I placed a box of matches and a candle by my bedside, and it was not long before we were both asleep, my last recollection being the sound of the dog's stertorous breathing; then a blissful, dreamless unconsciousness came over me.

A cold nose against my cheek, and two long nailed fore-paws vigorously scratching to get into my bed, awakened me quite suddenly, and I found my friend the fox-terrier standing on my chest, trembling most violently, and whining in a distressed fashion.

"You ungrateful little brute," I said angrily, giving her a far from gentle push on to the floor; but in a second she was up again, doing her best to get under the bedclothes.

"Not if I know it;" and again I sent her flying. The room was quite dark, and as the fire had been pretty bright when I went to bed, I guessed I had been sleeping some time.

Thoroughly enraged, when the dog jumped up for the third time, I threw her roughly down, and this time I heard her patter under the bed and creep into the farthest corner, where she sat trembling so violently that she shook my bed.

By this time I was thoroughly awake, and fearing I had hurt the dog, I put my hand out of bed, snapping my fingers to call her and make my *amende.*

My hand was suddenly taken into the grasp of another hand, a soft, cool hand, at a temperature perceptibly below my own flesh.

To say that I was astonished would but mildly convey my feelings! After a few seconds of steady pressure the other hand let go, and almost simultaneously I heard a heavy sliding fall, like the collapse of a large body at the foot of the bed. Then in the absolute stillness of the room there sounded a deep human groan, and some half-articulated words, or to be accurate, prayers.

The voice — if it could be called a voice — died away into another groan; the dog under my bed gave a sharp hoarse bark, and scratched and tore at the wainscoting. Fully convinced that some one in trouble of some sort had got access to my room — by what method I could not imagine — I struck a match and lit my candle, springing from the bed and crying out, "Who's there? What is it!"

My eyes blinked for a little at the sudden light, but when they were steady I looked to the spot where I had heard the groan. There was no one.

The room was absolutely empty, and exactly as I had left it on going to bed. Nothing was out of order, nothing was moved, and there was nothing I could see to account for the noises I had heard.

To make certain I tried the door. It was still locked. I made a tour of inspection round the walls, which were painted, not papered, examined all the furniture, and finally, kneeling at the foot of the bed, held my candle so as to be able to look underneath.

In the corner crouched the fox-terrier, but there was nothing else. The polished boards reflected the light of my candle, and perfectly mystified I was getting up, when I felt the hand I had been resting on the floor was damp.

I held it close to the light, and saw my finger-tips, and the ball of my thumb were reddened as if with blood, and turning back the rug I discovered a dark stain extending perhaps for two feet one way, and three or four the other.

Instinctively I looked at the ceiling, but its whitewashed surface showed no corresponding mark. Nothing had dropped from above. The stain was damp, not wet, and yet felt warm as though the fluid, whatever it was, had been recently spilt. I examined my finger-tips again. The marks were very like blood. Bah! I dabbled my hand in the water in my basin rather hurriedly, then I once more went carefully round the room.

The shutters were barred, the door was locked, there was no cupboard in the wall, and the chimney was still hot from the fire. I tapped the walls carefully and could find no indication of any hollow place that might possibly be a secret door, but as I did so my common sense revolted at my own folly; they were so innocent of any panellings or dadoes that could conceal an exit.

If a practical joke had been played upon me, where had the delinquent vanished to?

One hypothesis alone was possible, and that I indignantly rejected, for I knew I was wide awake in my sober sense and not the victim of delusion or waking nightmare.

For a minute I contemplated writing the whole thing down there and then, but the absurdity of the matter flashed across my mind. I looked at my watch and found it was nearly three o'clock. It was better to warm my shivering limbs in bed than chill myself further by writing what no one would believe, for after all I had seen nothing, and who would credit groans and whispered words without one particle of corroborative evidence? The fox-terrier's "mark" to the important document would not enhance its value in the eyes of the Psychical Research Society.

So I crept back to my nest, first enticing the dog from her corner, and in a half-acknowledged wish for company, even if it was only that of the little beast, I took her into bed with me.

I left the candle burning for a short time, then as there were no further noises, I put it out, and prepared once more to woo the drowsy god, and falling asleep was not disturbed again.

When I had finished dressing the next morning I — curious to see what was there — turned back the rug at the foot of the bed. Sure enough I found the dark stain, just as I had seen it in the night, with this difference — it was no longer wet, but appeared of long standing.

CHAPTER IV

We were to shoot some home coverts that day, and besides ourselves O'Connoll expected six guns, a few neighbours and a sprinkling of officers from the nearest garrison. Betty, too, took me on one side and told me that her friend of the dimples and dot was coming, and that I was to be sure and not let "dear" Captain Adair monopolize the young woman's attention, but that I was to "go in and win."

Miss "Dimples" arrived, also "dear" Captain Adair, a tall, dark ruffian who had basely forestalled me by getting the pretty little lady in question to drive him out. I found this warrior was a universal favourite, O'Connoll declaring that he was "one of the *few* decent soldiers" he knew; whilst Betty — well, Betty was sickening!

Adair and I were told off to a warm corner, where to my great joy I wiped his eye over a woodcock. He grassed two long-tails that I missed in an unaccountable manner, but every one knows one woodcock is of more value than many pheasants.

We had a capital day's sport, plenty of walking, and a most varied, if not very big, bag, as there were birds of all feathers about. As for the rabbits, the whole place walked with them, as one of the keepers said, they were indeed a "fright."

Betty and the Dimpled Damsel lunched with us, and followed the guns in the afternoon. Miss Dimples would have none of me, but tripped gaily after the all conquering Captain Adair, so Betty took pity on me.

"Did you sleep all right, really, Kenneth, last night?" Betty asked me anxiously, as we walked along together.

"Don't you think it likely?" I answered, looking hard at her. "Of course I did, all the same. But if it is convenient, may I be moved into a room facing west? My present quarters face east, you know, and I never sleep really well that way."

"Then you did see something," she said in a low voice.

"Not a thing," I answered cheerfully.

"Don't try to humbug me, Kenneth; I know you so well that it is impossible."

"Honest Injun! Betty, never one little ghostie on a postie did I behold." I spoke laughingly; the night was far off still. "But, to be strictly truthful, I did think I heard a groan or two, and though it probably was only my fancy, I would much rather not hear them again! By the way, is there any story connected with that room, anything to do with that stain on the floor?"

I saw her colour under my watchful eyes.

"Maurice said nothing to you about it, then?"

I shook my head.

"Well, people have complained before — in fact, we don't generally put any one there now. The room is called the Muckle or Murder Hole room, and the story goes that the stain on the floor is the blood of a man stabbed there by his brother. Two O'Connolls quarrelled over the ownership of the Castle, and fought, and the dying brother cursed the other, praying that no eldest son should inherit direct from his father. Maurice succeeded his grandfather, you know, and even he had an elder brother. I believe the curse has always been fulfilled. The room had been disused for fifty years or more when we did it up. The stain has been planed off the boards several times, but it always comes again — creeps up from below in a few hours; no one knows how. Maurice won't believe in any of these stories, having heard them all the days of his life. He declares that one person tells another, and then, nervous to begin with, of course they imagine a ghost. So, when you were coming, he insisted on your being put in there, for he said you could not be prejudiced by any nonsense, and that we would be able to prove what folly it all was."

I do not know that I altogether appreciated O'Connoll's kind experiment at my expense. However, I told Betty he was quite right, as no better man could be chosen to "lay "the ghosts.

"I'll have you moved to-night," my cousin continued. "Don't tell me what you saw" — I made a movement of protest — "or heard; for, Kenneth — don't laugh at me — but though I hate myself for my folly, I am often more nervous than I can say."

"You nervous, Betty! I am ashamed of you — why, what has come to you?"

She interrupted me quickly —

"I can't explain it. The only description which at all comes near the feeling is somewhere in the Bible, where it speaks of one's heart becoming water. I never felt the least fear when I came here, though, of course, I heard all kinds of stories, and have had all through endless trouble with servants leaving at a moment's notice, frightened into fits. When people staying here said they saw things I only laughed, and declared it was mere nonsense, and though we've always had quite unexplainable noises, such as the great chains of the front door being banged up the staircase and along the gallery, and endless footsteps, and sighing and cries, and rustlings and taps — they never frightened me. Even when sudden lights and tongues of flame, and letters of fire on the walls, came many times, both of us saw them, for Maurice did see them, too, though he hates to own it — I was only curious and annoyed because I could not explain it satisfactorily to myself. But, Kenneth, a year ago — last November — I saw 'It,' and I have never felt the same about these things since, or ever shall."

"November is the height of the season in your spooks' society?" I asked lightly, trying to cheer poor, serious Betty.

"Yes, nearly all the stories are about that month, though odd spirits appear all through the year. It's in November that there is said to be the vision of a dead troop of soldiers, drilling in the ring."

"What are your stock apparitions?"

"There are so many, I don't remember them always, but I will try and recall what have been seen within the last six years. First, of course, there is a banshee. She sits on the terrace, and keens for coming deaths in the family. Then there is Earl Desmond's ghost, who howls in a chimney, where he was hiding and got smothered. A monk, with tonsure and cowl, walks in at one window and out at another, in the Priest's House; that is the wing beyond the blue room, where I sleep now. He has been seen by three people to my own knowledge, not servants; for, of course, their stories are endless, and require more than a grain of salt. Then there is a little old man, with green cut-away coat, knee breeches, stockings, and bright shoe buckles, holding a leathern bag in his hand. Quite a dozen people have seen him. Sometimes he is all alone, sometimes a little old woman to match him is there, with skinny hands, long black mitts, old-fashioned dress, and a big head-dress, so they describe her. My mother saw them; and a third figure, an old man, dressed like a priest, with an intensely cunning face. She saw all three together several times."

"Do these ghosts do any harm, or talk to you, or anything like that?"

"The green old man tries to stop people, but no one has been brave enough to interview him yet. Then, in the Priest's House, comes a burly man, in rough clothes, like a peasant; he pushes a heavy barrel up the back stairs of the wing, near the servants' bedrooms, and when just at the top, the barrel rolls down, bump, bump, bump, a fearful noise, and all disappear."

I fear I laughed heartily at this inconsequent ghost; but Betty went on, unmoved —

"Then there is a woman with very few clothes, and a red cloth over her face; she screams loudly twice, and disappears. That is on the same landing as the barrel man. These have been seen by numberless servants, and —"

"My dearest Betty, do you mean to say you believe old wives' tales, told by the common or garden domestic?"

"No, I don't," said Betty candidly. "I don't mind about these one bit. I tell you, because I am trying to give a full catalogue of all who have been said to appear in my married life here."

"Go on, my dear."

"Then" resumes Betty, "there is a tall, dark woman, in the historical scarlet silk dress that rustles. She haunts the blue room, which used always to be the nursery, and sobs at the foot of the children's beds. My last nurse and two or three maids have seen her. Her story is that she was a poor soul one of the O'Connoll's kidnapped, and she had an infant soon after she was brought into the Castle, which O'Oonnoll threatened to kill if she would not marry him, and when she had yielded to him, he stabbed the child before her eyes, saying she could not look after him and the baby at the same time. They found her dead next day, having killed herself with the knife that slew her child."

"What nice, cheerful little ways the O'Connolls seem to have had."

"They were simply robber chieftains, and robbed and murdered without compunction," said Betty. "Then there is a scene on the gallery, seen once in my day, and several times in past generations. Some time in back ages there was a beautiful girl two of the O'Connoll men were attached to. Both often tried to abduct her — one at last was successful. The other brother, returning angry and disappointed to the Castle, found the girl was already within its walls. A violent quarrel ensued between the two men, in the middle of which the girl escaped from the room in which they all three were, and ran, shrieking, along the gallery. 'Let him who catches her keep her,' shouted one man, as they both started in pursuit. The original abductor caught her first, and, with a cry of triumph, lifted her in his arms.

"'Keep her then,' cried the brother; but as he spoke he ran his sword twice through her back and killed her. The whole scene is reenacted in the gallery."

Betty related this pleasing legend with much spirit.

"Oh, Betty," I cried, "do say there is a blue light. That story is nothing without a blue light."

"I don't know if the light is blue," she answered simply. "But the keep is lighted up, when this apparition is seen, for a minute. When the girl is killed everything disappears. I have seen the keep lighted up myself — once."

"How? When? And where?"

"Driving home from a day's hunting at the other end of the county — two girls who were staying here and myself. We were very late, and it was so dark I had to walk the horse up the avenue. When within sight of the Castle, I could see the yellow light of the lamps shining through the cracks of the shutters in the wing and from the hall. Of course, as it always is, the rest of the tower was in darkness. Quite suddenly there was a brilliant stream of white light from all the windows and arrow-slips in the keep — from the big chapel windows and all. I had just time to exclaim 'Oh! look at the light,' when it went out just as suddenly as it started shining."

"Some one taking a look round the place with a torch or something," I hazarded.

"No one would venture up the winding stairs to the chapel at that hour, I can tell you! Besides, I know no earthly light but electricity could produce the strong glare I saw."

"A sudden flash of lightning, probably."

"There was no thunder or sign of any. However, I never expect any one to believe it. I saw it — that is all I know."

"You tried to find out an explanation? "

"Of course I did," replied my cousin crossly. "Do you think I *like* having that kind of thing happen in a place I am to live in for the rest of my natural life, and my children after me? There, Kenneth, I did not mean to snap at you," she added penitently. "But when people talk as if they thought one went out of one's way to invent the very things which make life a burden, I *do* get annoyed. I *never* tell people these stories now, because they simply don't believe one;

81

or if they do, write one down a weak-minded, self-deceptive, backboneless idiot."

"Betty, you *know* that I —,"

"You are 'Kenneth' and not 'people' But to hark back to the ghostly inventory. There is something heavy that lies on people's beds, and snores, and they feel the weight of a great body pressing against them, in a room in the Priest's House, but see nothing. No one, to my knowledge, has seen whatever does this, only heard and felt it. Then there is something that very young children and dogs and cats see, but no one else. Fortunately, as the children grow out of babyhood they seem to lose the power of seeing this thing. My babies saw it when they were too young to talk, and were sent precious nearly into convulsions. My cats go quite cracked, spit, claw, and run up the curtains, and the dogs — oh! it was only a day or two before you came that Maurice and I were in the smoking-room with four or five dogs, when, without rhyme or reason, they all dashed into the hall, barking furiously! Then just as quickly they dashed back again, their coats bristling, their tails tucked between their legs, the picture of fright — old Oscar as bad as any of them. Maurice ran out, but could see nothing uncanny; yet no amount of driving or coaxing would bring the dogs out again; they crawled under chairs and sofas, shivering, and refused to budge."

"Could your husband make it out?"

"Not a bit. But that often happens. Those are all the ghosts I can remember in the house — except It. But outside they swarm. Really I am not surprised, for the whole neighbourhood was a veritable Armageddon. We cannot plough anywhere near without turning up skulls galore."

"Why don't you let the place to the Psychical Research people?" I suggested. "With such a delightful assortment of ghosts 'on tap,' they would be charmed to take it."

"I only wish Maurice would," said Betty, "or get some one to come here and investigate. But like all Irishmen he adores every stone and blade of grass that belongs to him, and he won't hear of the place being uncanny in any way. Once a friend wanted to send a parson with book, bell, and candle, to 'lay' a ghost she saw, and Maurice was furious; and when I suggested inviting a man I know who is very clever at probing into those kind of things, he would not hear of it! He gets so angry with the country folk when they refuse to come here after nightfall, and when they say the place is 'dark,' meaning bad. As for me, he thinks I am rapidly becoming fit for the nearest idiot asylum, because I am in such deadly terror of ever seeing 'It' again."

"Would you mind telling me what you saw yourself, Betty? O'Connoll told me you had had a fright."

"I'll tell you if you like, Kenneth, but of course you will find some plausible — and utterly impossible — 'natural' explanation for it. Maurice says vaguely 'it was after dinner,' which is extra rude, for I am, and always have been, strictly blue ribbon. Still, here are the facts. Remember, I do not expect you to credit one word! We had a party for shooting here last November, among others my sister Grace and one of my brothers — dear old Ted you know. Well, we had tramped with the men all day, so we were all tired and turned up to bed early. I went the round of the girls' rooms, then got into my dressing-gown and had my hair brushed, after that I sent my maid off to bed. Maurice and I were the only inhabitants of the red wing, next the room you slept in last night — no one else that side of the tower. I heard a noise in the hall, so went out on to the landing and along the gallery and looked over. There I saw Maurice putting out the lamps himself. He had a lighted candle in his hand, and was evidently just coming up to bed.

"'Maurice,' I called to him, 'will you bring me the last *Contemporary Review* out of the drawing-room please? I want to read an article in it.'

"'All right,' he called back, 'I am just coming up to bed.'

"He left one lamp burning, and went through into the drawing-room, whilst I, leaning my elbows on the corner of the gallery balustrade, waited for Maurice to reappear. I recollect I was wondering what kind of sport I should have the next day, when I was going to hunt with Mr. Blakeney.

"Suddenly, two hands were laid on my shoulders. I turned round sharply, and saw, as clearly as I see you now — a grey 'Thing,' standing a couple of feet from me, with its bent arms raised, as if it were cursing me. I cannot describe in words how utterly awful the 'Thing' was, its very undefinableness rendering the horrible shadow more gruesome. Human in shape, a little shorter than I am, I could just make out the shape of big black holes like great eyes and sharp features, but the whole figure — head, face, hands and all — was grey—unclean, blueish grey, something of the colour and appearance of common cotton wool. But, oh! so sinister, repulsive, and devilish. My friends who are clever about occult things say it is what they call an 'Elemental.'

"My tongue stuck to the roof of my mouth, and I felt every hair on my head separate and move — then the spell was broken.

"I wheeled round — fortunately outwards — on to the open gallery, and with something — not myself — in my throat that shrieked continuously, I tore along the passage, down the stairs, through the corridor into the Priest's House, where my sister was sleeping. Once in her room I nearly fainted; but, pulling myself together, I managed to make my husband and brother — who, hearing the shrieks, had flown to the rescue — understand that there was a 'Thing' in the gallery, which had frightened me. They ran up together, and searched carefully; but, though they hunted up and down, they found nothing. My brother just saw 'It' for one second, and you know he died. It is said to be a very bad sign of one's luck to see 'It.'"

Betty paused to wipe her eyes for a minute; then resumed —

"I soon got all right, though my teeth would not stop chattering for half an hour, and I told them quietly what I had seen. Maurice was dreadfully frightened at the time — now he declares I was hysterical, and that a cat jumped on my back!"

Betty had grown quite white as she related her adventure, but managed a smile as she said the word "hysterical."

"It must have been a trick, Betty!"

"Who could have played it on me, or who would be in that part of the house? I grant you it is *possible* some unknown enemy conceived the excellent plan of trying to frighten my few remaining wits away, but it's not very probable — and I who saw 'It' — oh! but what's the good of talking — I should like to explain it to my own satisfaction; but I can't. One thing I know, if ever I meet 'It' again I shall go stark, staring mad or die the very minute. Having no ambitions for Bedlam, I take every precaution to prevent such a fate overtaking me. I have forsaken that wing of the house, leaving those rooms for strong-minded people like you. Also, I make my maid sit in my room now until Maurice goes to his dressing-room. There, Kenneth, I have told you, and doubtless you think me an infinite fool — but, oh! Kenneth, if you had only seen 'It.'"

"Be assured, Betty, if I do, I will put a ˙450 revolver bullet into the cotton wool, and make the funny joker's inside sorry for itself — that is all I can say," — and I meant it.

Our talk drifted into other channels, and by the time the gathering twilight sent us indoors to tea and hot cakes, I was no longer thinking of the galaxy of ghosts that my cousin had trotted out for my benefit.

Betty and the "Admirable" Captain Adair, who was staying the night, sat after tea on the fender stool in front of the cheerful turf fire gossiping lazily, so Miss Dimples had perforce, in default of better game, to pay a little attention to me, and by the time the dressing gong sounded we were discussing mutual affinities, having reached this interesting conversational point by the chromatic scale of dancing, hunting, shooting, plays, books, religious beliefs (Miss Dimples would have been an aggressive Agnostic had she known how), first impressions, telepathy and palmistry (Miss Dimples told my fortune, making an amusing record founded upon the romances of a well-known military novel writer), thence to affinities; we agreed that the topic was not properly threshed out and should "be continued in our next."

I had been shifted, I found on going up to dress, into a room next the Murder-Hole chamber, and thought my new, bright, big quarters a distinct improvement. The floor was carpeted, and looked respectable and comfortable, and not suggestive of blood stains and murders. I looked forward to a real sound sleep that night.

We spent a merry evening; Captain Adair, who was staying the night, sang us comic songs until we ached with laughter, and Miss Dimples, smiling and fascinating, completed my subjection. Alas! I am not the owner, or ever likely to be, of those dimples and that dot.

After dinner we went out in a body to catch the half-past eleven ghost and to time the dogs. When we first neared the kennels there was a great deal of pleased sniffing and whining from the dogs, but, to the second correct, the wild howling began.

None of us could see what started the chorus, so that mystery remained unsolved, though we each tried our best to find plausible theories. After many songs, came whisky — when the ladies had gone to bed — shouting choruses is apt to make one thirsty.

Then we turned upstairs to our respective rooms, my little friend the fox-terrier, whose name I found to be "Nell," accompanying me again.

Tired out with the long tramp and sleepy from the extra glass of whisky those thirsty songs were answerable for, I knew nothing from the time my head was on the pillow until the servant brought my bath water next morning.

CHAPTER V

Miss Dimples was a laggard at breakfast. Betty was just going in search of her, when the door opened, and she came in. Her pretty rosy cheeks had lost their colour, and she looked quite pale and tired — as if she had not slept.

"What have you been doing?" O'Connoll asked, with much severity. "Reading a trashy modern novel in bed, eh, young lady! Or, like that sensible wife of mine, interviewing a ghost?"

No one could accuse Miss Dimples of being pale now — she flushed painfully, a vivid scarlet.

Betty looked at her with troubled eyes, and O'Connoll, seeing the effect of his jesting words, frowned wrathfully. I threw myself into the breach, talking fast and intentionally in a loud voice to my host as to the day's prospects.

When O'Connoll, taking Adair with him, had departed after breakfast to consult with his steward — an ubiquitous treasure, whose duties ranged between buying the babies' boots and arranging the various shoots, Miss Dimples, with many more blushes, broke the sad fact to her hostess that she was recalled home.

I was sorry for the poor child, for she was in an agony, between inventing a specious lie and not seeming in unseemly haste to quit her friend's roof.

"I am so sorry to go, dear Madam O'Connoll," she said, with telltale flaming cheeks, "but I got a letter from mother this morning, saying she is not very well, and that she wants me to come home."

Betty did not believe this story, nor did I; but as a very strong motive was evidently behind the girl's many excuses, I resolved to try and extract the truth.

It was arranged that Miss Dimples should depart after lunch, and Betty, jingling a huge bunch of keys in a workmanlike fashion, started "housekeeping," telling her friend to amuse me for half an hour.

"You've been telling terrible tarra-diddles, Miss Dimples," I said reprovingly, when we were alone, shaking a reproachful finger at the fair sinner. "You never had any letter this morning, but a very obvious bill forwarded on to you. I particularly noticed the blue envelope lying in solitary grandeur on your plate."

"If you did notice, you shouldn't have, and you are horribly rude to tell me to my face I tell stories. Those are Indian manners, I presume; now *dear* Captain Adair —"

Miss Dimples pouted in a provoking charming manner at me. "We are not talking of Captain Adair, damn it, I should say, bless him!" I interrupted austerely, "but are discussing the infamous conduct of a little lady, who, having told several very inartistic fibs within the last five minutes — by the clock — now refuses to confess and receive absolution."

94

"Certainly I refuse, with *such* a father confessor!"

"You will not find a more sympathetic one in all Ireland, including its garrison towns!"

An alarming glare from two heavily curtained eyes made me hasten to add: — "See, I am quite in the right attitude." I sank on my knees with my hands clasped. "Now, fair ladye, in your mercy tell your devoted knight what wicked monster disturbed your rest, that I may rend it limb from limb!"

"I wish you could," she answered with a frightened glance round. Then in more natural tones, "*Do* get up; don't be so silly. What would The O'Connoll think, if he came in? Don't be so silly!"

"People might imagine I was laying my heart at your feet. Shall I?"

"My shooting-boots might hurt the valuable article." She placed *en evidence* an absurd travesty of a "broad soled" boot. I could have held the two on one hand. "There, the lace is untied! As you are in a convenient position, will you tie it for me, please, Captain Gordon?"

"If I tie it so that it won't come undone again all day, will you tell me?"

The "shooting-boot" was in my possession, so I was not adverse to parleying with the enemy.

"Will I tell you what?"

"All about everything!"

"What do you mean? You make me shudder with your sweeping questions. Good gracious, no!"

"Then I shall unlace your boot."

I began to carry out my threat.

"You are horrid! Do it up again at once, and when it's quite done, I might begin to think of telling you something."

Philandering over a minute shooting-boot is very pleasant, but it was not business in this case, so with a smothered sigh I repaired the damage, and released the hostage, which disappeared to join its fellow under the leather-bound checkerboard skirt Miss Dimples wore as appropriate to sport.

"Now sit down — no, not here — over in that chair. Well, first you must swear by — by your spurs, not to tell The O'Connoll."

"I swear it."

"Or ever in a horrid club smoking-room."

"I never enter such places; my mama does not like me to."

"Or ever to tell Madam O'Connoll."

"May not Betty know?"

"Certainly not. It's bad enough my having to be as rude as I am in flying off like this, without my adding insult to injury by telling some stupid story about the house."

"So be it; I won't tell Betty then — just yet."

"I went up to bed, you know; you gave me my candlestick. By the way, I believe you made my fingers black and blue." She critically examined her plump little digits. Miss Dimples runs to entrancing hollows even in her hands. "No, stay where you are — you need not look at them, thank you. Only be more careful next time you hand a person a candlestick. Well, we talked a little, and brushed our hair, and drank some tea —"

"Do you women drink tea at that hour? What horrible depravity!"

"You men drink whisky, which is worse. Now if you interrupt me *once* again, I shall stop altogether, so there! Well, I went to bed, as I said before; my room is called the Clock Room, and it is in the Priests' House. I locked my door quite securely, but I could not sleep for ages, not a wink, though I was dreadfully tired from that awful tramp and my poor feet" — here the "Number two" shooting-boots peeped out pathetically, to emphasize her remarks — "simple *ached*. I heard all you men go to bed, a nice row you made! Then I heard the servants go past, making those elaborate efforts to walk

98

softly, which result in twice the noise of ordinary footsteps. Then I tried counting, but that woke me up all the more. At last I composed two new frocks, and the mental effort *did* make me drowsy, so I tried to recollect Dr. Monaghan's sermon — I was in Ballykinkope last Sunday, and that put me off in a few seconds."

"But, Miss Dimples, with your anti-religious convictions, do you go to church?"

"Of course I do. One must give whatever Protestant tenants one has a good example! Besides, at home I play the organ, and it's such fun composing the voluntaries. You can't think what a beauty 'The Absent-minded Beggar' makes!" She laughed merrily. "Now don't interrupt any more, or I truly will stop. Just as I was dosing off great heavy footsteps coming up the stairs woke me up again, heavy steps like a big labourer with clodhopping boots would make. I listened, thinking I was safe, as my door was locked, wondering who it could be. The footsteps came along the corridor and stopped at my door for a second, and then came on right into my room, as if no door was there at all! I can swear the door never opened, but the footsteps came right on through! It sounds very mad I know, but it's truly true, Captain Gordon. The footsteps went about the room for several minutes, and I nearly *died* of fright. I kept my eyes tight closed, afraid I might see something and expire, or worse still, my hair turn white in a single night! However, at last I could not bear the horrible idea of this thing walking about unhindered, and I got strength to open first one eye a teeny, weeny bit, and then both. It was quite light in the room, the turf of my fire had fallen in and was burning brightly. Well, I looked about, but could *see* nothing, yet all the time the heavy footsteps went on across the room to the wardrobe and back to the fireplace — the very boards creaking under the weight of — nothing that I could see! At last, to my horror, the footsteps came over to the foot of my bed, and the ghost — yes, it must have been a ghost, I am positively certain — sat down plump on the edge of the bed, almost on to my toes. It is a great, big, heavy ghost, too, for it made all the springs rattle. Fortunately, the bed in that room is very broad — one of those great, spreading, hospitable beds, you know, and I was lying away from the ghost, with only my feet over to its side; so gradually drawing my toes up — Heaven knows how I had courage — I crept softly out on the other side, and along the floor on my hands and knees into the corner behind my bath. The big felt mat the maid spreads for me to stand on was folded up there, and I wrapped myself up in it. There I sat all night shivering with cold and fright, whilst that horrible great big pig of a ghost lay on *my* bed and snored and snorted most comfortably. You may laugh, Captain Gordon — I only hope it will go to you to-night — I did not feel in the least like laughing, I can assure you. When the morning came, and it grew light enough to see, I looked over to the bed, fully expecting to see some hideous monster lying there; yet there wasn't a thing. My door was locked just as I had locked it; but on the second pillow — the one I had not used at all — was the impression of a heavy head, and all along the eider-down quilt there was the mark where the huge long ghost had lain. I would not sleep another hour in this house — no, not for a million pounds. It's not at all kind of you to jeer at me, Captain Gordon, for I am quite in earnest; and really and truly I was utterly unnerved and never so frightened before in all my life."

I did my best to comfort the poor little girl, who evidently enough had imagined an exceedingly alarming experience, which whether bred in her own nerves, or caused by some spiteful sprite, had succeeded in making her pass a very miserable night. She was quite shaken, and had only just escaped a bad cold, as the result of her night out of bed, and was not at all fit for the fourteen Irish miles she must drive before she got to her own home; but in vain did I urge her to delay her going until the next day. She was stubbornness itself, and as the very suggestion of spending another night in Kilman seemed to give her pain, I refrained from further pressing, and led our conversation into lighter, less nightmarish channels.

O'Connoll and Adair joined us after a bit, and then Betty with a cloth cap over her eyes, and a light 20-bore in her hands.

"I'm one of the guns to-day," she announced airily.

"No, you don't, Betty," replied her husband. "I'm not going to have murder committed on my land, if I can help it. Put that popgun away, if you are coming with us. If you must shoot to-day, you may go by yourself; not with the rest of us, if I know it."

"Oh! Maurice —"

"It's no good, my dear. Didn't you take the toe off my boots a few weeks ago, shooting rabbits out of the oats? "

"The shot did not go within a yard of your boots, you teasing storyteller."

"Quite near enough to ruin my nerve for the rest of the day, anyhow. Here, put up that gun, like a good girl, and help beat to-day. Betty always thinks if she taps an occasional tree, she is doing wonders. You'd shoot a beater for a moral certainty, and times are too bad now for me to be able to afford you 'big game.'"

"I've been out dozens of times," his wife replied, with an injured air, "and wiped your eye before now."

"I daresay," said her husband drily. "I've had many marvellous escapes, I will own.

But since the corn-cutting — no, thank you. 'Once bitten, twice shy.'"

"Very well," said Betty, resigning her gun. "I will beat to-day; but to-morrow, Kenneth, you and I will go out together, and you will see what sport we will have."

"If women *must* shoot," remarked O'Connoll dictatorially, "and nowadays they are not happy unless they do everything we do — and lots of things we would be ashamed to do — then let them make up their own parties, and shoot each other. There are plenty of superfluous women about."

Miss Dimples rose immediately to his insulting bait.

"You men are just jealous," she declared. "You know, O'Connoll, your wife is a capital shot! Of course, we women do everything better than you men; and in shooting we score, because we have not sat up half the night making our hands shaky with whisky!"

"What about tea" I began, but a fiery glance quelled me.

"I've known some pretty shots amongst ladies," said the diplomatic Captain Adair.

"My sister is a first-class shot," Betty remarked, — "much better than I am. How we laughed at her this summer, though. We used to go out with a little repeating rifle, stalking rabbits, and at first she would start out with a silk-lined skirt and frou-frouey petticoats, that the rabbits could hear rustling a mile off. But plenty of women shoot now — and well, too. There's Lady Garry Owen, who is a champion at woodcock, and Lady East Riding knocks down all before her. And do you remember the American widow at the Chenistown shoot last year, Maurice? She showed you men the way."

"With a huge cigar forever in her mouth, and the tightest of tight rationals on. I should just like to see you doing it, Betty." O'Connoll laughed at the recollection of the Transatlantic dame. "Well, come along, here are the others — we must hurry up."

The morning's sport was as varied and excellent as the shooting of the day before. The pheasants were nearly all wild birds, and were mighty strong on the wing. We walked over the most different land — bog, covert, marsh, and heather succeeding each other in pleasant variety.

Besides pheasants we massacred a few snipe and many woodcock; also the usual plethora of bunnies. Hares we saw, but O'Connoll preserves them strictly for Mr. Blakeney's sporting pack of harriers which hunt in the neighbourhood. Betty promised me a day with them.

After lunch came a tender parting with Miss Dimples. She was kind enough to express a hope we might meet again, and murmured comforting assurances that she would keep me some dances at a ball, coming off within the next ten days.

I never knew if Miss Dimples did keep those dances for me! Anyhow I fear that lucky beggar, Adair, got the benefit of them; for events crowded, and sent me back across the silver streak long before the ball came off.

CHAPER VI

Adair left Kilman after dinner that night.

He came into my room, when I was changing my shooting things, and began to chat.

"What a rummy old place this is," he volunteered. "You never were here before, were you? There are no end of stories going round about ghosts, you know. Not that I believe in such yarns, do you?"

"You never found a moderately old place people did not say was haunted; and as Kilman is immoderately old, of course they are bound to call it so," I answered sententiously.

"Yes; but sometimes you do hear most unexplainable rows here. Why, only last night, I'd have sworn some one was singing in a big cupboard there is in the room I was given."

"Practical joking, I should say."

"I don't know how it was done, all the same, as I searched the beastly place out several times; but no sooner did I get to bed again than the infernal music began once more."

"It's to be hoped your visitor had a pleasing voice," I laughed, at his injured tone.

"The song, if I could call it a song, was wordless — all a jumble of vowels, sung on a succession of minor notes, always ending in a particularly piercing tone that gave me a pain behind my eyes, and made me want to sit up and howl like a dog. I feel sure those poor brutes last night heard the same thing when they yelped. Oh! of course it's all rot. I daresay I dreamt it; but I thought I'd ask you if you had dreamt it, too. One doesn't like to ask O'Connoll about the matter, for, though he is the best of good chaps, yet he's a bit touchy on that point. I remember once he was very near knocking my head off, because I hinted at something being wrong in another room I was then in."

I assured Adair I had not had "the mysterious minstrels" in my room, and asked for particulars of his other experiences.

"Mind you," he began, "I don't believe in ghosts, not for a second; yet it is funny, I must own. What happened before? Oh! nothing much; only every time I got into bed I was rolled out again. Mind you, I saw nothing, though I looked pretty smartly, I can tell you — with a candle in one hand and a revolver in the other — only, as I told you, no sooner did I lie down again than the mattress humped itself up and threw me."

"A bucking mattress is a new and added terror to the history of ghostology."

"I pulled the bally old bed to bits, and at last yanked it all out on to the floor, where I slept in a heap. The man who called me thought me quite mad, or very drunk. However, I told him I could not sleep any other way, and cleared that day. O'Connoll would not believe a word of the matter — of course, he did not tell me in so many words — but he laughed, and patted me on the back, and advised me to have four, instead of three fingers of whisky next time, and then I would sleep better. Madam O'Connoll laughed, too; but promised she would never put me in that room again, and never has. All the talk of spirits is folly; but this is a very rummy place, there's no doubt about that!"

With this he left me, and when he had gone I regretted that I had not asked him if, by any chance, it was in the room I was now in he had been so rudely disturbed; but my mattress, as I punched it, seemed incapable of any such Buffalo Bill tricks. When Adair had departed, after dinner, we talked shooting. I told shikari tales, and romanced over the tigers I had nobbled, giving the full account, from start to finish, of the exciting sport I had had with the late owners of two fine pelts I was giving to my cousin.

Half-past eleven came and went, heralded as before by the dogs; but in going over the stories of past hunts and big shoots, we took no heed of time. It was past twelve when

110

Betty left us, and nearly one o'clock before we thought of turning in. O'Connoll rang up a servant, and asked him if the house was shut up, and the household gone to bed.

"They have," said the man.

"Then you can go, too — I will put out the hall lamp," answered his master. "Now, Gordon, we'll have one more drink, and then make for bed."

We walked into the hall, and O'Connoll showed me the old fashioned locks and heavy chains that barred the doors, I mentally wondering how these chains could be taken from their staples, and dragged and rattled upstairs in the way Betty had described. Then he put out the lamps, and with "Nell," the fox-terrier, at my heels, and a favourite cat of his following him, we walked upstairs.

He saw me into my room, gave my fire a poke and made it up, then, wishing me good-night, walked across the gallery to his dressing-room, and I heard him open and shut the door.

Left for the night, my first action, as it always is, was to lock my door. Then I put a candle and matches near my bed, and prepared to make my little friend "Nell" a comfortable corner.

The dog and I had grown allies. Betty said she was quite jealous, for "Nell" was a faithful old lady, who did not generally admit new loves into her doggie heart.

"It's one of Betty's tests with new people," O'Connoll told me. "If 'Nell' does not growl at them, they are all right; if she does, nothing will persuade Betty that they are not burglars in disguise, and she will have nothing to say to them."

I threw my rug down again to-night for "Nell," who sat in front of the genial blaze, and turned her damp nose up to me in the trustful way that dogs have.

Wheeling a low roomy armchair into a good position for the light of the lamp to fall on my paper, I got my writing-book, and, with my legs each side of the fireplace, began to write some letters which it was absolutely necessary should leave by the next day's mail. Up to the present I had really had no time for writing, but now it was business and had to be done.

My first letter was to a firm of naturalists who were setting up some markhor heads and bighorns for me, telling them to send two good specimens and a couple of tiger skins on to Kilman; next I wrote to my gunmakers about an express rifle I was in treaty for.

Pausing only to light my pipe — I can never get my ideas to run straight without the aid of my old briar — I began a long and rather intricate letter to my lawyer, about a monetary matter that had been giving me a great deal of bother lately. Stooping to replenish the fire — the one drawback to these delightful turf fires is the constant need there is of putting on fresh sods — I looked down to see where the dog was, for I missed her from my feet.

"Nell" had disappeared.

I whistled softly and snapped my fingers. A faint tip, tip, tip, tip of a wagging tail told me her whereabouts. The fox-terrier had hidden under an old secretaire in the corner, and had no intention of coming out. I called her repeatedly, with no result.

"Don't be such a little fool," I said crossly, kneeling down and pulling her out by the scruff of her neck. "You are not going to begin fresh pranks, I trust."

"Nell's" big brown humid eyes looked wistfully into mine, but the moment I relaxed my hold, she attempted to creep back under the secretaire again. However, I prevented her, and carried her to the bed I had made for her by the fire.

Then I was just settling down to my writing again, when a scratching at the door caught my attention.

I looked up to listen; the terrier gave a veritable scream of terror.

The dog was sitting bolt upright on the rug, every hair of her coat bristling roughly, her lips drawn up, showing her brown old teeth, her ears laid back flat to her skull, her eyes fixed on the door, trembling with the same painful rigours of the night she had first been my companion.

The noise at the door continued. At first I fancied some cat or dog was trying to get in, but then I noticed that the scratches kept up a kind of time — one, two; one, two, three; one, two; one, two, three.

I set my teeth. The unknown exponent of the art of practical joking at Kilman had chosen the wrong time for a display of his pranks.

He was safer when he kept to the darkness of midnight. Suddenly awakened out of sound sleep in a black Egyptian gloom, a man is not so formidable a foe as when with a lamp lighted, candles burning, and fire blazing, he catches up a revolver that has often proved its accuracy, and goes forth to inflict condign punishment on the villain or fool attempting to frighten him. I was enraged at the dastardly way poor Betty had been tricked, and resolved that if "he," "she," or "it," who were guilty of these disturbances would only show, they would regret the hour that they tempted their fate.

My revolver was soon taken from the holster case, in which I carry it about. I assured myself that it was loaded, then walking across the room I unlocked the door and flung it wide open.

There was no one outside.

The landing and corridor were empty, and beyond, through the half-open door that divided the wing from the tower, I could only see the blackness of the unlit gallery. When I listened, my straining ears seemed to catch the sound of a soft thud, then a rustle, then another soft thud going along the gallery; but as I could not see, I turned quickly into my room, and catching up the candle from the table at the side of the bed, walked out on to the landing, and through the door into the gallery, holding the candle overhead, and striving to pierce the dark depths below and around me.

All was still now; only my own breathing broke the silence. I sniffed the air — faugh! a subtle, unknown, and horribly vile smell filled my nostrils, and sent me back quite sickened to my room. There was no more to be done, so I shut and locked my door, and turned with a sigh to my bothering letter.

"Nell" welcomed my reappearance with rapture and every demonstration of delight. She jumped on to my knees, and tried to cover my face with her frenzied kisses. I felt that she was still trembling violently, so I soothed and petted her for a few minutes before putting her back into her bed.

I had scarcely taken up my pen again, when a noise came from the far end of the gallery — thuds and brushings. Whatever caused the noise advanced right up to my door, and fell or threw itself once or twice heavily against the framework. Then the scraping began again — one, two; slow and long scratches right down the panel. One, two, three; shortly and quickly succeeding each other; then a rustling or brushing noise against the door, followed by another thud and more scratching.

I sprang up, sending my papers flying in all directions, rushing to the door, unlocking it and tearing it open. The same sickening smell struck my nostrils; the mat that lay across the threshold was half turned back;

but beyond this there was no more to be seen this time than before.

But most unmistakably I heard the rustling, brushing, soft dumping noise at the end of the gallery!

Should I walk across and rouse O'Connoll?

This would entail waking Betty, and her being left alone whilst I carried off her husband to help in the hunt for this mysterious night-bird which was disturbing me. I was the only occupant I knew of the red wing, the O'Connolls alone in the blue wing, and in the Priests' House were the babies and servants.

Should I cross the gallery, I debated, go through the blue corridor, down the stairs and into the Priests' House, in search of the butler?

I had no kind of idea which was his room, and my endeavours to discover him might land me in nurseries with terrified shrieking babies and irate nurses, or in the women servants' quarters, where indignant and hysterical maids would call down vengeance on my devoted head.

Even should I succeed in finding the man's room, what should I ask his aid for — a burglar hunt?

But burglars do not scratch with their finger-nails on people's doors.

A ghost hunt?

Then I should probably frighten all Betty's domestics into departing next day, besides laying up endless ridicule for myself when nothing came of it. How did I know that Oscar, the deer hound, had not been taught the clever trick of scratching and bumping in correct time?

There was nothing for it but to go back and await further developments.

I shut the door, but did not lock it, put my papers away, all idea of further writing being out of the question, placed the lamp on a chest of drawers exactly opposite the door, lighted every candle in the room and revolver in hand, stood by the door ready to wrench it wide open before the practical joker could have time to depart.

The first intimation of the return of my visitant was, as usual, from "Nell," the fox-terrier. Again her coat bristled and her limbs stiffened, the same visible tremor shook her whole body, and her eyes once more fixed themselves with agonized attention on the door.

In a little, I, too, heard the bump, bump, bump, along the gallery, the rustling and brushing, the thump against the door. Then a sniff under it, and a long scratch, as if with a sharp fingernail, down the paint.

Breathless with excitement, I flung back the door.

In a moment I knew what Betty had meant when she said her hair "moved." For my flesh all over my body and scalp crept, and every hair on my head stood straight on end.

I must admit without reserve that I was utterly terror stricken, and absolutely paralysed with fright! My hand holding the revolver dropped limply to my side when in the full glare of the lamp I saw the Creature that squatted in the doorway.

No one who has not experienced the sensation can in the smallest measure understand the absolute weakness that came over me, the seeming cessation of the pulses of life, the grip in heart and brain, the deadly numbness which rendered me incapable of thought, word or action, when I first saw that awful beast.

I heard a sharp yelp from the terrier just when the door swung back, but after that there was no further sound or movement from the dog, and the Creature on the mat and I faced each other in absolute silence. The lamp burnt brightly, the fire fizzed and puffed and my fascinated eyes took in every detail, every gruesome feature, of the indescribable Horror squatting at my door.

The Thing was about the size of a sheep, thin, gaunt and shadowy in parts. Its face was human, or to be more accurate, inhuman, in its vileness, with large holes of blackness for eyes, loose slobbery lips, and a thick saliva-dripping jaw, sloping back suddenly into its neck! Nose it had none, only spreading, cancerous cavities, the whole face being one uniform tint of grey. This, too, was the colour of the dark coarse hair covering its head, neck and body. Its forearms were thickly coated with the same hair, so were its paws, large, loose, and hand-shaped; and as it sat on its hind legs, one hand or paw was raised, and a claw-like finger was extended ready to scratch the paint.

Its lustreless eyes, which seemed half-decomposed in black cavities, and looked incredibly foul, stared into mine, and the horrible smell which had before offended my nostrils, only a hundred times intensified, came up into my face, filling me with a deadly nausea. I noticed the lower half of the creature was indefinite and seemed semi-transparent — at least, I could see the framework of the door that led into the gallery through its body.

I cannot tell exactly how long we thus stood, gazing at each other — time seemed to cease and eternity begin — but at last the creature gave a species of hop and landed well inside the room.

Then my hitherto nerveless fingers closed round my revolver — oh! the comfort its cold stock gave me — and covering the Brute carefully between its prominent eyes — I fired.

A crash of lead striking the wood of the large hanging cupboard *behind* the object I aimed at, told me I had either missed, or my bullet had gone clean through the Thing's head. *It* did not seem one bit inconvenienced, merely turning its vile countenance at the sound of the splintered wood.

I took aim once more, desperately determining that if lead could solve the mystery, my bullet should this time.

I *could* not have missed, but another ping of the bullet into the wardrobe was the only result of the second shot.

My flesh crept again, and a stifling tightness clutched my throat. Either my eyesight was failing, or the Creature was gradually becoming less distinct. Just as I was preparing for a third shot, it reared itself upright, and holding its arms rather bent it took one step forward, as if about to spring upon me.

Was it the trick of my hot aching eyes or not? I cannot say, but the horrible bestial lines of the Creature gradually merged into the grey, featureless shape Betty had described.

Overcoming the strongest physical repugnance at the thought of the Creature touching me I pressed my revolver right up to or *into* its breast — and fired! Springing back to avoid its "hands" clutching me my ankle twisted, and I fell, something striking me a sharp stinging blow on the temple.

CHAPTER VII

The next thing I heard was Betty's voice saying joyfully, "He is coming to, now, doctor, I am sure."

My eyelids seemed weighted as with lead, but with an effort I opened them, to see a man I could not recollect having ever met, standing over me with a pair of scissors in one hand and a roll of sticking plaster in the other.

Beside him stood Betty, and Maurice was supporting my head. I was lying on a bed in a small room I had not been in before, but which, from the whips and boots about, guessed rightly to be O'Connoll's dressing-room.

"You fell and split your scalp open against an iron bed post, old man," said Maurice. "We got Dr. Charterly out to mend you up."

"Not quite as bad as that, O'Connoll," the doctor corrected, smiling. "I expect Captain Gordon has had many a worse head than this. There, that's as neat a job as I can make of it; you'll have to wear your hat well over your eyes to hide the 'plashter,' or your friends will say you've been prize-fighting. Want to get up, do you? I would not if I were you, it's not much more than seven yet, so lie where you are until breakfast-time, and try and get a sleep. Here, drink this up."

"Betty," I called rather weakly, feeling an insane desire to cry, "Betty, are you all safe?"

"Of course, Madam O'Connoll is. Why wouldn't she be?" interrupted the doctor. "It's ruining her complexion, she is, stopping out of bed like this. Now, O'Connoll, please, I'll be much obliged if you and your good lady will leave me alone with my patient. With your permission I will take a couple of hours' rest in this fine chair and then invite myself to breakfast with you, for I'm due at your dispensary at ten, so it's not worth while going home."

My cousin pressed my hand, and she and her husband left me alone with the doctor.

I was beginning to speak when he stopped me. "Look here, Captain Gordon," he said, "I presume you want to get well fast? Then don't be bothering your poor battered brain with thinking. You've had a fall and a fright — no one else was frightened or hurt, and you yourself are not at all bad; if you sleep now, you'll be well when you wake up."

"Doctor," I cried, earnestly, "I must get to Dublin to night, and Madam O'Connoll —"

"And Madam O'Connoll and himself are to go with you — by medical orders!" the doctor said, with a comical twist of his face." I'm hunting the lot of ye away for a change, babies and all. So unless you want to be left here all alone with the alternative of Ballykinkope Union Infirmary, get to sleep and be fit for the journey."

He sat in an armchair, wrapped a rug round his feet, and vouchsafed me no more words. My thoughts were confused and chaotic; but before I could arrange them the medicine he had given me did its work, and I went to sleep.

O'Connoll was sitting in the room when I awoke, and a tray with breakfast things was on a table beside my bed.

My head was quite clear now, I was free from aches and pains and very hungry.

"The doctor said you could get up when you'd eaten something. But there is no hurry, Gordon, as our train does not go until three o'clock. Feeling pretty fit again?"

"I'm so awfully sorry, O'Connell," I began. He stopped me.

"I know what you mean, old man; it's no fault of yours, I suppose. Look here, though, about last night. It's Betty I don't want to have frightened, for it would only make her worse at frightening people like she doubtless frightened you. All her fault again, of course."

"What happened when I fell? I suppose you heard my shots and came in?"

"You let fly three times, didn't you? I didn't hear the first shot. Betty did, and awoke me just at the second. I was half across the gallery when you fired last."

"Then you saw —"

He cut me short.

"My dear fellow, I saw nothing: I make a point of *never* seeing anything in this house. I simply cannot afford to! My father, grandfather, and their fathers before them, spent their lives here — deuced long ones, too, judging by my grandfather's. The ghosts were talked of then just the same, and no one was one bit the worse for them that I ever heard of. My idea is, if you leave them alone, they will leave you; so I have not seen, and do not see, and never *will* see one of them. But with my wife, it is different! So Gordon, I want you to help me — do tell her a good thumping likely lie, and make her think you were drunk."

"Kenneth can economize that lie," Betty said gently. She had heard her husband's last words as she came into the room. "I know what you are talking about, and I know Kenneth was not dreaming, and of course I know he was not drunk. But I don't want to know or hear another word on the subject. We'll stop in Dublin until November is over and then — then we'll come home. I am so sorry, Kenneth, that you have proved to be one of the small percentage who — 'see.' Many, many people come here, see nothing, and scoff at the idea of there being anything to see. You were less lucky. Now I'm going to pack up. Don't you go into the other wing again; the clothes you want will be brought you here, and the rest packed up. Now be a sensible man and don't go trying to remember about last night" (as if there was the smallest danger of my forgetting it), "but eat up your breakfast before you move."

"Betty's right," said O'Connoll. "We won't talk of ghosts again. After all, what is the good? It all leads to nothing."

"Where is 'Nell'?" I cried, suddenly thinking of my little terrier friend.

"She is dead," O'Connoll answered shortly, and I did not ask for more particulars.

Made in the USA
Coppell, TX
06 March 2021